Harry Potter
and the Prisoner of Azkaban

 by

J. K. Rowling

Scholastic Inc. grants teachers permission to photocopy the designated reproducible pages from this book for classroom use. No other part of this publication may be reproduced in whole or in part, or stored in a retrieval system, or transmitted in any form or by any means, electronic, mechanical, photocopying, recording, or otherwise, without written permission of the publisher. For information regarding permission, write to Scholastic Inc., 555 Broadway, New York, NY 10012.

Written by Linda Ward Beech
Cover design by Vincent Ceci and Jaime Lucero
Interior design by Grafica, Inc.
Original cover and interior design by Drew Hires
Interior illustrations by Mona Mark

Jacket cover from HARRY POTTER AND THE PRISONER OF AZKABAN by J.K. Rowling.
Published by Arthur A. Levine Books, an imprint of Scholastic Press.
Jacket art © 1999 by Mary GrandPré. Jacket design by Mary GrandPré and David Saylor.

ISBN 0-439-21115-8
Copyright © 2000 by Scholastic Inc.
All rights reserved.
Printed in the U.S.A.

Table of Contents

Before Reading the Book

SUMMARY

Harry is in his third year at the Hogwarts School of Witchcraft and Wizardry. However, things aren't quite as they used to be at Hogwarts: A prisoner, Sirius Black, has escaped from the dreaded Azkaban and is trying to get into the school so that he can kill Harry. Guards from Azkaban known as dementors surround Hogwarts, and Harry is forbidden to leave the grounds. The students enjoy their Defense Against the Dark Arts classes with a new professor, Remus Lupin; but only Harry, Ron, and Hermione seem to appreciate Care of Magical Creatures, taught by their friend Hagrid. Harry uses a secret map to sneak through a tunnel to Hogsmeade, where he overhears talk about his dead parents. Black succeeds in breaking into the school a few times, and security is tightened. Harry and his friends finally learn the surprising truth about Black: He was a friend of Harry's parents, was wrongly imprisoned for killing 13 people, and is Harry's godfather. The real villain is Peter Pettigrew, imprisoned in the body of Ron's pet rat, Scabbers.

CHARACTERS

People

Harry Potter . . . . main character
Lily and James Potter . . . . Harry's parents
Vernon and
Petunia Dursley . . . . Harry's uncle and aunt
Dudley Dursley . . . . Harry's cousin
Aunt Marge . . . . Uncle Vernon's sister
Albus Dumbledore . . . . . headmaster of Hogwarts
Professor
Minerva McGonagall . . . . Transfiguration teacher
Voldemort . . . . Lord of Darkness and Evil
Madam Poppy Pomfrey . . . . school nurse
Rubeus Hagrid . . . . . . Hogwarts groundskeeper
Professor Remus J.
Lupin . . . . Defense Against Dark Arts teacher
Ron Weasley and
Hermione Granger . . . . Harry's close friends
Arthur and Molly Weasley . . . . Ron's parents
Percy, Fred, George, Bill, Charlie . . Ron's brothers
Ginny Weasley . . . . Ron's sister
Neville Longbottom, Seamus
Finnigan, Dean Thomas . . . . Harry's friends
Draco Malfoy . . . . Hogwarts bully
Lucius Malfoy . . . . Draco's father
Crabbe and Goyle . . . . Malfoy's friends
Colin Creevey, Parvati Patil, Lavender Brown,
Lee Jordan . . . . Gryffindor students
Ernie Macmillan . . . . Hufflepuff student
Professor Severus Snape . . . . . . Potions teacher
Professor Sprout . . . . Herbology teacher
Professor Flitwick . . . . Charms teacher
Madame Hooch . . . . Flying teacher
Mr. Argus Filch . . . . Hogwarts caretaker

Sibyll Trelawney . . . . Divination teacher
Oliver Wood . . . . . . Gryffindor Quidditch captain
Alicia Spinnet, Katie Bell,
Angelina Johnson . . Gryffindor Quidditch players
Marcus Flint . . . . Slytherin Quidditch captain
Cedric Diggory . . . . Hufflepuff Seeker
Cho Chang . . . . Ravenclaw Seeker
Pansy Parkinson . . . . Slytherin student
Penelope Clearwater . . . . Percy's girlfriend
Cornelius Fudge . . . . Minister of Magic
Stan Shunpike . . . . conductor of Knight Bus
Ernie Prang . . . . driver of Knight Bus
Sirius Black . . . . prisoner of Azkaban
Peter Pettigrew . . . . friend of James Potter
Macnair . . . . executioner
Dementors . . . . Azkaban guards
Tom . . . . landlord of Leaky Cauldron
Madame
Rosmerta . . . . . . proprietor of Three Broomsticks

Ghosts

Peeves, Nearly Headless Nick

Animals

Hedwig . . . . Harry's owl
Scabbers . . . . Ron's rat
Mrs. Norris . . . . Filch's cat
Fang . . . . Hagrid's dog
Errol . . . . Weasleys' owl
Trevor . . . . Neville's toad
Ripper . . . . Aunt Marge's dog
Crookshanks . . . . Hermione's cat
Grim . . . . giant dog; death omen
Buckbeak . . . . hippogriff

ABOUT THE AUTHOR

For J. K. Rowling, writing is her greatest pleasure. She wrote her first book (still unpublished) at the age of six. Says Rowling, "I have always written, and I know that I always will; I would be writing even if I hadn't been published." J. K. Rowling got the idea for the Harry Potter books while on a train from Manchester to London. When she began writing the first Harry Potter book in a café in Edinburgh, Scotland, Rowling was on welfare with an infant daughter. Helped by a grant from the Scottish Arts Council, Rowling took five years to finish, *Harry Potter and the Sorcerer's Stone*.

During that time she was also planning the six sequels, one for each of Harry's years at Hogwarts. Says Rowling, "It was my life's ambition to see a book I had written on a shelf in a bookshop."

Rowling is a graduate of Exeter University and a former teacher. In addition to the British Isles, she has also lived in Portugal. Her favorite holiday is Halloween, when she holds a big party for her friends and their children.

LITERATURE CONNECTIONS

Other books by J. K. Rowling:
• *Harry Potter and the Sorcerer's Stone*
• *Harry Potter and the Chamber of Secrets*

VOCABULARY

Students might be unfamiliar with the following words. Write the list on the chalkboard. Have each student look up two or three words, and then write the meanings on the board. Then have students each make a tic-tac-toe board that contains nine words from the list. Read aloud in random order nine definitions from the chalkboard list. Each time students hear the definition for one of the words on the grid, they cover that word with a slip of paper. The first student to complete a row across, down, or diagonally wins, provided that he or she has matched each word with the correct definition. Play again using other words from the list. Students can exchange grids for further rounds.

mundane	pompous	ballistic
levitate	tirade	aura
sallow	euphoria	sabotage

luminous	shards	tirade
fez	wastrel	turbulent
amber	apoplectic	opaline
contemptuously	podium	marauder
pompously	divulge	ballistic
furtive	levitate	sabotage
cavernous	insolent	extricate
dilapidated	sallow	debris
tumultuous	apothecary	abysmally
placidly	mundane	pirouette

aura	apparition	hallucination
manic	bandy	derisively
shrewdly	taunt	clairvoyant
undaunted	insufferable	euphoria
vindictive	convulsively	revulsion

NOTES ABOUT GENRE

Point out that some books of fiction fall into the category of fantasy. List on the board the following characteristics of fantasy:

- Events in the story could not happen in real life.
- The story is often set in a place that doesn't actually exist.
- The characters use special powers or fanciful strategies to solve problems.

As students read the story, have them identify ways in which *Harry Potter and the Prisoner of Azkaban* fits the definition of fantasy.

GETTING STARTED

Try the following strategies as you introduce the book to the class.

- Display the cover and invite students to comment on the animal that Harry is riding. What do they think it is? What might it be called? Why are he and Hermione on it?
- If students read *Harry Potter and the Chamber of Secrets*, what do they recall about Azkaban? Who was imprisoned there before? Who do students think the prisoner will be in this book?
- Invite students to leaf through the book and note chapter headings, illustrations, and different typefaces. Ask: What kind of story do you think this will be? Why?

TEACHER TIP

Have students write predictions about the story in a writing journal. After they read the book, ask them to share their predictions and compare them to what actually happens.

Exploring the Book

CHAPTERS 1–7

WHAT HAPPENS

Harry loses his temper when Aunt Marge speaks disparagingly of his parents. He runs away from the Dursleys and is picked up by the Knight Bus, an emergency transport for stranded witches and wizards. He learns that Sirius Black, a prisoner in Azkaban fortress, has escaped. According to the conductor, Black murdered 13 people and was a supporter of Voldemort. At Diagon Alley, Cornelius Fudge, the Minister of Magic, arranges for Harry to stay at the Leaky Cauldron pub. Soon, his friends Hermione and the Weasleys join him. Harry overhears Mr. and Mrs. Weasley say that Black wants him dead. On the train to school, Harry and his friends sit with the new Defense Against the Dark Arts teacher, Professor Lupin. The train suddenly stops, the lights go out, and a dementor appears at the door. Harry hears screaming and passes out. At Hogwarts, the students learn that dementors are guarding the school from Black. In Hagrid's class, Malfoy is scratched by a hippogriff named Buckbeak. In Lupin's class, the students learn to use a charm against a boggart.

QUESTIONS TO TALK ABOUT

COMPREHENSION AND RECALL

1. Why does Harry try to blackmail Uncle Vernon about permission to go to Hogsmeade? (*It's the only way he'll get his uncle to sign.*)

2. Why can't Harry control himself in front of Aunt Marge? (*She says mean and untrue things about his parents.*)

3. Why does Mr. Weasley think Black is after Harry? (*Harry stopped Voldemort; Mr. Weasley thinks Black wants Voldemort back in power.*)

HIGHER-LEVEL THINKING SKILLS

4. Why does Harry want to do his summer homework? (*Possible: It connects him with Hogwarts; he likes school.*)

5. Why is Fudge willing to bend the rule about underage wizard magic for Harry but not the one about Hogsmeade? (*Possible: He believes Harry is in danger.*)

6. How is Harry's reaction to the dementor different from his friends' reactions? (*They are all cold, scared, and upset, but Harry goes rigid and faints. He also hears voices.*)

7. Why doesn't Hermione like Professor Trelawney? (*Hermione likes facts from books; facts can take her only so far in Divination.*)

8. Why do you think Professor Lupin doesn't give Harry a chance to face the boggart? (*Answers will vary. He may be protecting Harry.*)

LITERARY ELEMENTS

9. Character: How does Harry show his feelings for Hagrid? (*He volunteers to go first with Buckbeak. He and his friends comfort Hagrid after Draco is hurt; they say they'll stand up for him.*)

PERSONAL RESPONSE

10. Laughter is the best way to repel a boggart. What else is laughter good for? Why do you think so?

11. What shape would the boggart take for you? How do you usually face this fear?

12. Harry and his friends miss the Sorting. Suppose you were there. Which house would the hat send you to? Why?

CROSS-CURRICULAR ACTIVITIES

MATH: *Gringotts Gold*
Have students assign a monetary value to each of the coins that Harry Potter and his wizard friends use: gold Galleons, silver Sickles, and bronze Knuts. Then have students price some of the things for sale in Diagon Alley, such as the books, Gobstones, and the Firebolt. Students can then work in pairs to make up problems for classmates to solve.

ART: *The Best Broom*
Review different types of ads with students; for example some ads use statistics to wow consumers, others use testimonials, some use the bandwagon approach (everyone's doing it, so should you), and still others use snob appeal. Encourage students to find examples of different types of ads in magazines. Then challenge students to create a magazine ad for a Firebolt.

WRITING: *Monster Minibooks*
Remind students that Hagrid assigns students the *Monster Book of Monsters* to read for his Care of Magical Creatures class. Encourage students to use their imagination to write a monster story in minibook form. Suggest that they illustrate their books.

My Book of Monsters

TEACHER TIP

At the beginning of the book, Harry is so determined to do his homework that he reads in bed under the covers with a flashlight. Use this example to initiate a discussion of homework strategies. Ask students where they prefer to do their work. What motivates them to do it?

WHAT HAPPENS

Hermione's cat goes after Ron's rat causing friction between the two friends. Harry feels left out when the other third-year students all go to Hogsmeade. The Fat Lady is slashed and vanishes from the portrait through which Gryffindor students enter their tower. Everyone is on the alert for Black. In a Quidditch match against Hufflepuff, Harry sees the dementors and faints again. His Nimbus broomstick is destroyed. Lupin promises to help Harry fight the dementors. The Weasley twins give Harry a map, which shows him how to get from Hogwarts to Hogsmeade. There, he joins Ron and Hermione for some shopping. At the Three Broomsticks, Harry learns that Black was his parents' friend and their Secret-Keeper, but he betrayed them. He also learns of another friend, Peter Pettigrew. At Christmas, Harry gets a Firebolt from an unknown giver. In a Quidditch match against Ravenclaw, Harry uses his Patronus to get rid of some dementors who turn out to be Draco and his pals. Ron wakes up yelling one night when Black gets into the dorm. Hagrid has to take Buckbeak before a committee to defend his behavior. Harry sneaks off to Hogsmeade again, but this time Draco sees him. Snape catches Harry and takes away the map.

QUESTIONS TO TALK ABOUT

COMPREHENSION AND RECALL

1. Why is the Fat Lady so upset? (*Sirius Black slashes her when she won't let him in.*)

2. What memory comes back to Harry when he sees the dementors on the Quidditch field? (*He's aware of his mother saving him from Voldemort and dying in his place.*)

3. How does Professor Lupin describe dementors? (*They take every good feeling and happy memory; they make a person soul-less.*)

4. Why doesn't Azkaban need walls to keep in prisoners? (*They're all trapped in their own heads; can't think of a single cheerful thought.*)

5. Why does the first trip to Hogsmeade upset Harry? (*He learns that Black was his father's friend who eventually betrayed his father.*)

HIGHER-LEVEL THINKING SKILLS

6. What does Lupin mean when he says "what you fear most of all is fear. Very wise, Harry"? (*Harry's afraid to be afraid because fear weakens him.*)

7. Why is Quidditch so important to Harry? (*He excels at it.*) How does it represent his life at Hogwarts? (*He is the Seeker; one who is looking for the Snitch and also one who is looking out for evil in the school.*)

8. Why is Ron so upset when Crookshanks gets Scabbers even though the rat is wasting away? (*It's his pet; he has happier memories of it; he doesn't like the idea that the cat can hurt something of his.*)

9. Why is it irresponsible of Harry to go to Hogsmeade? (*He knows it's dangerous and that other people are worried about him. He's taking advantage of secret things—the map and his invisibility cloak.*)

LITERARY ELEMENTS

10. Character: When Professor Snape catches Harry with the map, how does Harry act? Does he behave like a wizard or a boy? (*He lies, gets angry, and tries to cover up. He behaves more like a boy than a wizard.*) How else could Harry have acted? (*He could have been truthful, owned up to his pranks, been polite, respectful.*)

PERSONAL RESPONSE

11. How does Harry feel about being left behind when the other students go to Hogsmeade? Have you ever been in a similar situation? Describe it.

12. What happy memory would bring a Patronus for you?

13. What would you say to someone in a Howler if you were really angry with him or her?

> ### TEACHER TIP
> Help students recognize the word patron in *Patronus*. Ask: "How is a Patronus like a patron?"

CROSS-CURRICULAR ACTIVITIES

SCIENCE: *Star Charts*
Remind students that Harry, Ron, and Hermione make star charts for Astronomy. Encourage students to find books with information about the stars and then make their own charts. Students may wish to include the names of constellations on their charts.

ART: *Signs of Hogsmeade*
Students can have fun designing appropriate signs for the different shops and other places in Hogsmeade. List the following on the chalkboard for students to select from: Zonko's Joke Shop, Shrieking Shack, Dervish and Banges, Three Broomsticks, Honeydukes, post office. Encourage students to make signs that reflect what the places sell or represent.

WRITING: *Fates and Fortunes*
Students might pretend they are members of Professor Trelawney's Divination class and write fortunes on slips of paper. Put the fortunes in a bowl, mix them up, and have each student take one to read.

WHAT HAPPENS

Buckbeak is sentenced to be executed. Harry and the Gryffindors win the Quidditch cup. Professor Trelawney predicts that Voldemort's servant will soon join him. Ron finds his missing rat in Hagrid's milk jug. The truth finally comes out: Black did not betray Harry's parents and has been imprisoned unjustly. In fact, he is Harry's godfather. Peter Pettigrew, imprisoned in the body of Scabbers, was the murderer and follower of Voldemort. Lupin is a werewolf, and Snape has been giving him potions to keep him from changing at the full moon. Harry prevents Black and Lupin from killing Peter because he knows his father wouldn't have wanted them to become killers. Somehow, Pettigrew gets loose, and the dementors catch Black. Harry uses his Patronus charm and saves Black. Harry and Hermione use her Time-Turner and go back in time to save Buckbeak from the executioner. Buckbeak takes Black to a safe place, and Dumbledore tells Harry that his father is alive in him.

QUESTIONS TO TALK ABOUT

COMPREHENSION AND RECALL

1. When and why was the Whomping Willow planted? (*It was planted when Lupin came to Hogwarts as a student. It was a way for him to be smuggled out of the castle into a tunnel under the tree when the moon was turning full and he was becoming a werewolf.*)

2. Why did Harry's father become an Animagus? (*so he could turn into an animal and be with Lupin when he was a werewolf*)

3. Why does Snape hate Lupin and Black so much? (*He was jealous of them as a schoolboy. Black played a trick on him and he felt he'd been made a fool of, and he thought Lupin knew about it.*)

4. How did Black recognize that Scabbers was Peter? (*He saw in the newspaper photo that Scabbers was missing a toe; the only thing ever found of Pettigrew's after the explosion was a finger.*)

HIGHER-LEVEL THINKING SKILLS

5. In what way were Harry's father, Peter, Sirius, and Remus like Harry and his friends? (*They were young, thoughtless, wanted to have fun, and misused their powers.*)

6. Why doesn't Harry let Black and Lupin kill Peter Pettigrew? (*He doesn't think his father would have wanted them to become killers.*) Do you agree with Harry's decision? Explain.

7. What is Harry's Patronus? (*a stag like his father's*) How does he use it at the end of the story? (*to save Black, his godfather*)

8. Is Harry influenced by his professors? Which ones? (*Possible: Lupin who teaches him about the Patronus; McGonagall who is head of the Gryffindors; Dumbledore, whom he admires.*)

LITERARY ELEMENTS

9. Motive: Why is it that Hermione is the one who slaps Draco Malfoy across the face? (*Possible: She has a keener sense of fairness than the others. She helped Hagrid prepare the defense of Buckbeak. She's overwrought from taking so many classes.*)

PERSONAL RESPONSE

10. Many of the Quidditch players are constantly trying to get away with moves that are against the rules. Do you think this is true in all sports? Explain.

CROSS-CURRICULAR ACTIVITIES

LITERATURE: *An Old Story*

Remind students that Professor Lupin is a werewolf. Point out that the Latin word for *wolf* is *lupus.* Then ask students to find out where Lupin's first name, Remus, comes from. Tell students to look for the Roman myth about the twin brothers Romulus and Remus. Questions students can address include: Who was the real mother of Romulus and Remus? What happened to her? Who rescued the boys and nursed them? What did they accomplish as young men?

SCIENCE: *Animal Antics*

Several characters in the book, including Harry's father, are Animagi and can transform themselves into animals. Have students imagine that they can do the same. What animal would they be? Why? Ask students to do a brief report on the animal and explain what characteristics led them to choose it as their Animagus.

ART: *Cheering Charm Cards*

One of the questions on an exam in Harry's Charms class is about the Cheering Charm. Discuss with the class what it takes to cheer someone up. Point out that sometimes people send greeting cards to cheer up a friend. Have students design their own "Cheering Charm" cards. Suggest that students include pop-up pictures, hidden messages, or secret codes with special potion recipes for a secret friend.

Summarizing the Book

PUTTING IT ALL TOGETHER

Choose from the following activities to help students summarize and appreciate *Harry Potter and the Prisoner of Azkaban.*

CLASS PROJECT: *Hogwarts News*

Have students create a school newspaper for Hogwarts. Assign or have students select roles such as reporter, editor, proofreader, photographer, artist, cartoonist, typesetter, and so on. Decide how many pages the paper will be and what kinds of features to include. You might assign an editor to oversee each page. Then have students create articles, editorials, features (for example, a sports page or a menu for a feast), cartoons, and ads based on the events in the book. Remind students that a little magic or wizardry would be appropriate in a Hogwarts newspaper.

GROUP PROJECT: *Creature Chart*

Have students work in groups to make illustrated charts of the unusual creatures mentioned in *Harry Potter and the Prisoner of Azkaban* (for example, grindylow, kappa, flobberworm, hippogriff, boggart, Red Cap, banshee, ogre, hinkypunk, were- wolf, manticore). Point out that while some of these may appear in other literature, many sprang from the imagination of J. K. Rowling. Suggest that students use her descriptions as well as their own imaginations to illustrate these creatures. Students might include other data on their charts, such as what the creatures eat or where they live.

PARTNER PROJECT: *What Do You Say?*

Have students work with partners to prepare interviews with different characters in the book. One partner takes the role of a character, and the other is the interviewer. The questions asked by the interviewer should be based on events in the book. The student playing the character must answer the questions as the character in the book might. Some students may want to imitate the character's voice as well. Have each team conduct its interview in front of the rest of the class.

TEACHER TIP

Encourage students to think about the names of the charms. Many of them include Latin words. What do these words mean? How do they relate to the charms' power?

INDIVIDUAL PROJECT: *Spinning a Story*
Use the reproducible worksheet on page 16 as a writing assignment. Students can spin and then write about the topic they land on. You might have them spin and write more than once. Or use the worksheet as an oral assignment and have students spin and tell.

EVALUATION IDEAS
Provide a set of rubrics to use in assessing one or more of the summarizing projects. For example, a rubric for the creature chart might include these objectives:
• Did students organize the chart well?
• Did students utilize information from the book as well as their imaginations to illustrate the creatures?
• Did students illustrate the creatures in an original way?
• Did students show care in their execution?

Answers for Reproducibles
page 14: 1. The Knight Bus, emergency transport for stranded wizards, shows up and takes him to Diagon Alley. 2. Professor Lupin gets rid of the dementor with his wand and gives Harry some chocolate to help him recover. 3. Fred and George Weasley give him the Marauder's Map, which shows secret tunnels to Hogsmeade. 4. Words appear on the map telling Snape to mind his own business. 5. Harry conjures up a powerful Patronus to get rid of them. 6. Harry and Hermione use the Time-Turner to go back in time and save Black and Buckbeak.
page 15: Students' answers will vary. They may suggest the following traits: loyal, honest, hard-working, angry.
page 16: Students' answers will vary.

Prickly Problems and Fanciful Solutions

Harry and his friends face some interesting problems in the book. Often the solutions are amazing and magical. Write the solution for each of the problems on the chart.

Problem   ## Solution

1. Harry runs away from the
Dursleys and has nowhere to go.   _____
                                                              _____

2. Harry faints when a dementor
comes into the train compartment.   _____
                                                              _____

3. Harry doesn't have permission
to go to Hogsmeade.   _____
                                                              _____

4. Snape gets the Marauder Map
from Harry.   _____
                                                              _____

5. The dementors surround Harry
and Hermione as they try to
save Black.   _____
                                                              _____

6. Buckbeak has been executed, and
there's no chance of overturning
Black's sentence.   _____
                                                              _____

Name: _____

Harry's Character

What is Harry Potter like? Use the chart below to describe him. Be sure to include evidence from the book to support your choices. The first one is done for you.

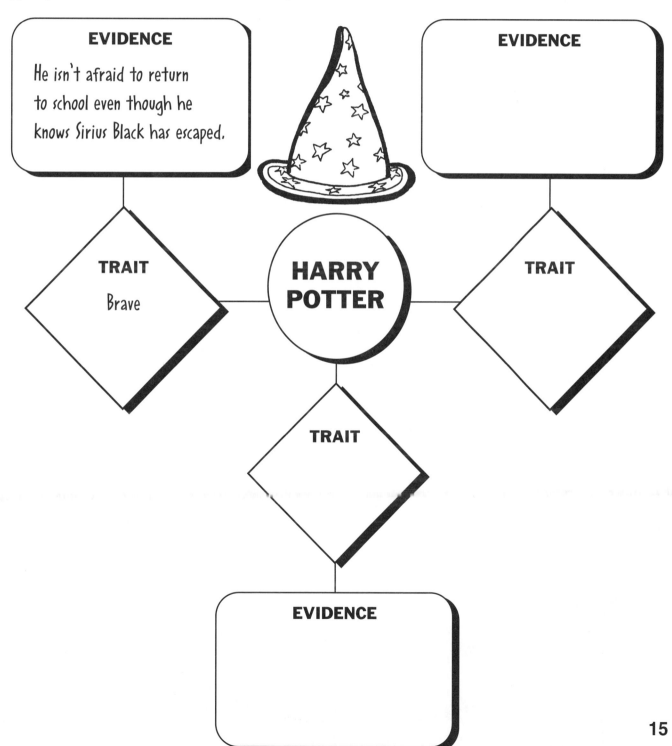

EVIDENCE

He isn't afraid to return to school even though he knows Sirius Black has escaped.

EVIDENCE

TRAIT

Brave

HARRY POTTER

TRAIT

TRAIT

EVIDENCE

Name: _____

Spinning a Story

Use a fastener to attach a paperclip to the middle of the circle. Then spin the paperclip. Read the words that you land on. Tell about that part of the story.

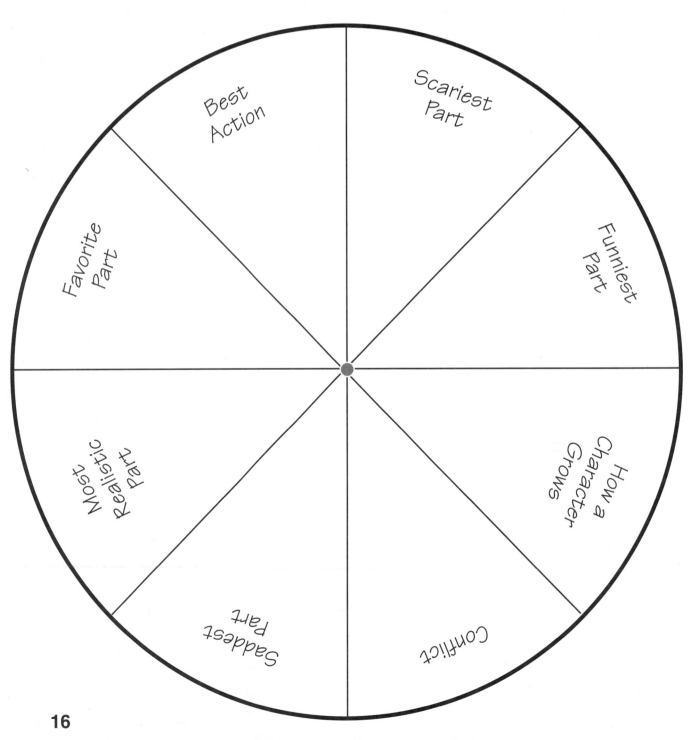

Scholastic Literature Guide • Harry Potter and the Chamber of Secrets